God of Branding:
Using a Podcast to Build a Powerful Personal Brand

Jeremy Ryan Slate

Table of Contents:

1. The Power of Thinking Big: Do You Dream Anymore?
2. Why You Need a Digital Brand
3. Why You Need a Personal Brand
4. Personal Brand: An Ancient Example
5. What Can a Podcast Do For Your Personal Brand?
6. Starting Your Podcast
7. How to Reach Anyone, the Tried and True Method
8. The Podcast Production Checklist
9. Tops Ways to Repurpose Content to Broaden Your Reach
10. Podcasting Tools for Success
11. Podcasting Gear to Sound Like a Pro
12. Finding Meaning in Success

1

The Power of Thinking Big: Do You Dream Anymore?

"The biggest obstacle to wealth is fear. People are afraid to think big, but if you think small, you'll only achieve small things."
                    -T. Harv Ecker

It seems to me that it's something that a lot of us can't figure out. And let me tell you, over my journey, that's been the idea as well. I think as entrepreneurs we just don't fit in a mold, we just literally can't. Someone tells us what to do, and we think the opposite, we just cannot do it. It's not that we have to be people that shake the bedrock of society, though some of us can, rather we do not do well with orders.

We want to do our own thing and we want to create, but I think in the midst of all that figuring things out, there can be a lot of action that takes us in a direction that we do not quite understand, that we can't quite feel the purpose of.

On my podcast, I've spoken to a ton of entrepreneurs that have had that same experience, recently, I got into this discussion with Keith Yackey, found of Amplify Live, on the podcast, and it brought that thought back to the forefront of my mind's awareness. There were days early in my business that I stared at a wall out of fear, but was able to pull myself out, because I was able to remind myself of why I was doing it. You can't be afraid to dream, in fact, you have to.

We deal with people that think we are bums, they see the work but they don't acknowledge it, because they can't accept what we are saying and just don't see the results that we claim to want so badly. This can be the toughest part, that's why working out our goals in writing is more something for us rather than for others, you most likely won't change these individual's minds. Keep your goals written, so after they hit with weapons of mass negativity, you can pull yourself out of the muck, or decide if you need their interaction at all. You'll be surprised what weeding certain people out of our lives will do for our well being a positive outlook.

The answer for almost all of us is getting a clear idea of what our purpose is, but it's just something that a lot of us don't get together in well-arranged fashion. We feel something inside that pushes us forward, but we never put voice to it, and let me tell you unless you do, you'll never get to a destination, there isn't a place of arrival unless you put it there.

Thought is a powerful thing; it created the Internet, the iPhone and brought man to flight. In our minds, it is the only place that we are truly free to create, because we do not have the restrictions of the physical universe. Thought comes before any action, even something as simple as deciding to move your foot. Create it first then figure out how you can do it. You'll find that we're amazing beings, maybe we will think things that technology can't make yet, but it will; that's how innovation happens.

You can never get too old to dream, and that's what we are as entrepreneurs, but those of us that can't put the action behind it are the ones that fail. That's why I started the Create Your Own Life podcast, to create life as an artist, but to put the action behind it to actually make it so. Don't listen to the naysayers, don't be afraid to dream, keep your goals ahead of you, you can't get to a destination without a map.

This may not be your story now, but you can remember a time early in your business when it was. You've always been the big thinker, something that was outside of the box, and once you were successful others marveled at what you had done. Though naysayers, many claimed to have expected the success all along.

Small goals are average goals that will probably never be reached. Goals have to big, they have to be huge. Why? To change anything about yourself you need some motivation, what better way to motivate yourself but with your actual goal.

In the pursuit of any goal, there will be trying times, and if a goal is not large enough, then it is very easy to walk away from, mainly because it did not create that internal motivation. A goal needs to be so huge that it makes you drool; it creates something in you that makes achieving your goal a life or death situation. Success cannot be treated as some little thing, but it is the only thing.

That massive goal is going to motivate you and push you toward it, gravitating all your senses.

Let's put it this way, would you rather come up short on making one thousand dollars or one million dollars? The choice here is easy, but if your goals are not big enough, you will not act big enough. If you want to change or create a higher purpose, then your actions and goals must meet; big actions and big goals.

Success just breeds more success and there is no shortage of how much success can be had. There's enough to go around. So, start making bigger goals, and start acting bigger to get to them.

I bring you back to this place, and emphasis the level of action, before we talk about how you can build a personal brand how successful it can be, because I want to bring you back to the magic. Thinking big is a magical thing and when you do it without reservation so many things can happen.

We will focus on a podcast as the center vehicle to personal branding here, because I feel that it has the ability to really create a big effect and bring that "big think" to a realization. Do I hope that some of you hire my company, Slate Media Productions, to do so? Absolutely. I know that we can really help you to create that effect.

However, this volume is something that you can walk away from and really put into action to start building a brand for yourself.

2

Why You Need a Digital Brand

"Today, getting people to hear your story on social media, and then act on it, requires using a platform's native language, paying attention to context, understanding the nuances and subtle differences that make each platform unique, and adapting your content to match."
-Gary Vaynerchuk

I had no right to be recognized, but had the will to do it and now in this new era of right now, media, I can make a name for myself, and thus help others to achieve what they want to happen as well. It's funny because in starting my podcast, I had no personal brand or following, but was able to have a ton of success because I got my central ideas down into succinct personal brand.

Business owners that already have a product or an established business have no idea how much of a leg up they have on me and the gold mine that they are actually sitting on. The real fact that they are missing to keep them from becoming a household name is the real engine and a message to blast out into the universe that will resound and help them reach people that just weeks before had no idea who they were.

We have reached a time period in the digital age where everyone is a brand and it doesn't matter if you are selling insurance or you're mom, hanging out at home baking the cookies. So, it is really important to have brand awareness, in that you have to constantly have in mind what you are trying to convey to the listening, reading or viewing world. Information can come at the snap of a finger, but so can annoyance; what will you be known for?

If you've followed Gary Vaynerchuk for a while, you are well aware that the current brand driven media is all about what type of value that you can give. You can't keep asking before you are giving and to simplify it, the formula is more like: give, give, give, give NOW ask. It's something out there you have to think about. We have reached this time period where everyone wants to be famous, but no one what's to put in the time to give value and to educate others and how their lives can be improved.

I find that every time I have a consult with someone about a podcast and PR program, I redirect them to Gary's book, Jab, Jab, Jab, Right Hook, because it really is the best existing resource out there to help create powerful content. It's not the main line of my business and to really get how "native" content on each of these platforms should look, you need to check it out.

Business owners should read this for the reason that initially all content will be driven by them as the goal setter. The plan will be eventually to have someone else do it, but if that person does not know what you unique voice and content sounds like then it will lose the opportunity to sound authentic and will get lost in a wasteland of digital information.

You not only need to be always giving value, but you also need to be cognizant of what image you are showing people in all times and in all places. There is so many ways to reach people, but then again, our world is noisier than ever; will you rise above the noise? Therefore, be careful what you posting on your social media platforms, as it will always be around. Sure as hell don't, play Facebook games, that's one way to get a lot of people to ignore you very, very fast.

With a digital brand, you can start out as no one, and very quickly build a network and a following if you show your face to the world as someone that is willing to give value; the exchange will balance itself out, if you continue to give people will want to give back to you. As an established person or brand, your rise can be even faster with the correct programs, staff and allotment of the marketing budget.

Stew on that for a moment. Now, what value will your brand give the world? Pick one thing, not ten, pick one, and offer the best possible content towards that can to that ends. A brand is one centralized thing, so start with what you do, you may do other things. But they are not relevant just yet and may be a big confusing. That is unless you are already well known in those other spheres, then it will take some well trained blending to make it all work and look seamless.

So like Simon Sinek says, "Start with Why," and then figure out how you will convey it to the public that you must attract. Get your message straight A digital brand is a long-term deal, but one of the most important that you will ever do, and will pay you back for the rest of your life.

Start correctly, take big actions, and have a plan of where you want to take it. BUT, remember, like Gary Vaynerchuk says:

Jab, Jab, Jab, Right Hook. You have to give a lot to get a lot, but in this digital world, anything is possible, even if right now, you're a nobody. If you're someone now, you can be bigger than you ever imagined.

3

Why You Need A personal Brand

"A brand is the set of expectations, memories, stories and relationships that, taken together, account for a consumer's decision to choose one product or service over another."
  – Seth Godin

Recently, we started a personal brand and podcast program for a very successful doctor. He works as one of the top practices in the country in addition to being a recognized author and successful business consultant. As individual businesses, the success is great and high level, but putting a personal brand behind them can be like jet fuel.

In this case, it meant creating a central website that organized everything that he is working on into one place, but also making them more available to members of the media in addition to being less confusing to the public.

Personal branding helps to unravel what you are all about; maybe it's your specific area of expertise or even a quirk about you. It's a combination of that, and also putting it all together to make sense.

It's also about casting a widening net, in the terms of creating a lot of content. Content for your own site, and also finding publications that may find you or your unique area of expertise valuable. This process can be very long depending on how often that you create content; there are a few unicorn occurrences when a single piece of content will jump-start someone on the road of success, but for the most part it's about creating content over and over again.

You may have picked up this book thinking you know how to podcast, and you most likely do, but I want you to look at this whole look from a point of view of building a personal brand. Even if you have been podcasting for some time, selecting this viewpoint will change how you operate and also change the results that you achieve from the end

In terms of branding, a podcast can do a lot of things for you and your company. I'll say first that, you'll see more as we go along, that I recommend that everyone do an interview type show. Unless, you have a lot of content that is already popular, then it will be an uphill battle to get noticed.

In addition to that, interviews do a fantastic job of positioning. Meaning that when people think your guests they think of you. It will also allow you to have the guest's help to promote when a show launches, allow for cross pollination and also changing the flow of your podcast; it's a help to your guest, yourself and most importantly to your audience.

Interviews are also important because it allows you explore someone else's content, because creating unique content on the level that is required for a podcast can be a bit more of a task than many entrepreneurs are open to. Interview style podcasts also allow for networking in a very different way than is typically possible. When you interview someone, you always have something to offer in publicity.

Besides the pure value that the interview itself offers, I end every interview with "Is there anything I can do for you and your brand?" It makes your service even more valuable, and how's how much you are willing to give. The important point here, that I have trouble getting across to people, is that you are not giving purely for the reason to get, but rather in the "Rising tide lifts all ships" type of way. I have built my personal brand entirely off of my willingness to give. The success of others does not detract from yours, but on the contrary it actually adds to it.

Become a giver and you will really create value for yourself and your company. It's a mind shift that some will never make, but it is a truly amazing thing when you make it your way of operating. You will be on your way to building a powerful game, and it will start to feel more like a game; significantly more fun!

4

Personal Branding: An Ancient Example

Positioning and personal branding is something that has been around for a long, long time. In actuality, it was used by the ancient Roman ruler, Caesar Augustus, to create the idea that he was a God, just by observing his father Julius Caesar and Pompey the Great's competition to be loved by the Roman people. The following is a trimmed down version from a Roman History volume that I wrote to show an extreme example of what branding and positioning can do for your personal brand.

While I find this to be enthralling and a great example, you may be one of those people that doesn't like history, in that case, I suggest you move to chapter 5.

Branding Like a God
The Branding of Pompey the Great as a God came about, somewhat indirectly, from the influence of Alexander the Great. The establishment of a cult to the Greek general led to a similar cult being established for Pompey outside of Rome; Pompey was shrewd enough to encourage this practice in the city of Rome itself. Pompey was portrayed as, and perhaps even thought of himself, as the Roman Alexander. Plutarch, for example, in his *Life of Pompey* states that Pompey was called Magnus (the Great) as well as resembled Alexander from youth.[1] The Roman general followed his Greek predecessor and personal hero in all things, and at times it could be argued

---

[1] Plutarch, *Life of Pompey*: 2.

that he even exceeded Alexander's accomplishments.

Pompey sought connections to Alexander for himself, and historical sources also connected Pompey with the Great. In his military career, Pompey came close to matching the exploits of Alexander, by conquering portions of Africa, Asia and Europe. During his Triumph of 61 BC, Pompey is rumored to have worn the robes of Alexander. The connection to Alexander is ultimately one of the most important steps in the process of appearing to be God for politicians at Rome, and although Pompey was the most adept at imitating and adapting Alexander's divine cult for himself.

The Value in a Super Bowl Parade
Pompey was considered to be the greatest *Roman General* until of course the actions of Caesar who triumphed four times, more than any Roman in history. A Triumph is like a Super Bowl parade on steroids for a victorious Roman General. Pompey's triumphs, even though he had less than Caesar, are arguably greater

because he conquered "the entire world."[2]

Pompey's first triumph was celebrated under unusual circumstances during the period of rule of Sulla, a Roman leader who was by most accounts literally insane. It was actually the insane ruler Sulla that granted Pompey the name *magnus,* meaning *great* in Latin. Therefore, just like Alexander the Great, he was now Pompey the Great.

Pompey chooses to have elephants pull his chariot in the triumph of 79 BC. Historian, Mary Beard describes the honors taken by Pompey to be too much, the elephants were taking the act too far, and were much too large to enter the city.[3] Less than a century later, Pompey's extravagance became acceptable. Romans seem to have easily forgotten this at the time of Caesar's 46 BC triumph, for which he used white horses in order to pull his chariot. These horses were an attempt by Caesar to claim divine status; the white

---

[2] It has been thought that Camillis triumphed four times, but Beard, believes this not be true. Beard 2007: 15. The known world during Pompey's time was Europe, Asia and Africa; Pompey triumphed over all three.

[3] Beard 2007: 236.

horse associated him with Jupiter, the sun god.[4]

Pompey's third and final triumph is his most important. He conquered not only territory that Alexander did, but he expanded on that territory: Europe, Africa and Asia saw the conquest of Pompey. This triumph followed upon Pompey's unique assumption of *imperium infinitum* ("infinite power to command") granted to him in 66 BC and extended until 63 BC. Originally intended for a period of six months to allow Pompey to rid the Mediterranean of pirates, it was extended so that Pompey could "settle the East" (that is, parts of modern Turkey, Syria, Israel, and the Greek islands. Alexander did not expand into Africa as Pompey did through his conquest of the pirates plaguing the Mediterranean; he was attempting to appear better than Alexander ever did. This is an edgy and dangerous branding move because it actuality he is not really better than Alexander, but he's hoping the Roman people do not notice that.

---

[4] Beard 2007: 234-5.

Three giant tablets were carried in the triumph parade, upon which were written the names of those over whom Pompey was triumphing. The triumph also coincided with Pompey's September birthday.[5]

Pompey attained the cloak of Alexander due to his conquest over Mithridates, who allegedly received it from Cleopatra VII. Yes, that is the well-known Cleopatra; if you weren't aware there were 6 Cleopatra's before her. She was the last ruler of the Ptolemaic dynasty of Egypt, the last of the of the kingdom's run by Alexander's generals to be conquered by Rome. Cleopatra's possession of Alexander's cloak is understandable, since the cult of Alexander started with his general Ptolemy, and his body was kept in Egypt after its theft by Ptolemy.[6] Pompey is supposed to have worn the cloak in his triumph. Besides this fact, the General in Triumph, in this case Pompey would also

---

[5] Beard 2007: 9.

[6] Beard 2007: 13-4, Zanker 1992: 10.

dress as Jupiter, the Roman King of the Gods.

Pompey's triumph for settling the east and ridding the seas of pirates was celebrated in 61 BC and lasted for two days, as opposed to the traditional single day triumph.[7] It was grander and bigger than all that had been before it. Prisoners were also an important aspect of the triumph, though it was not always easy to capture the enemy king alive. All of the soldiers and the enemy kind would also be part of the parade in chains, this effect was supposed to show how powerful the enemy general was.

The chariot used in the triumph was largely ceremonial; by the time of the Late Republic they were no longer use for warfare by the Roman army. As a result, they were specially contracted for the triumphant general. In and of itself, the triumph would be a powerful image, but special effort is given to make the chariot of the triumphant general seem more glorious.

---

[7] Beard 2007: 9.

In one of Pompey's three triumphs 61 BC, the chariot stands out for another reason. Although we know Pompey's chariot was expensively decorated, chariots were otherwise cheap in construction and offered a bumpy ride, making a triumph uncomfortable, and even potentially difficult for older generals; even a healthy person stood in a triumphal chariot with difficulty.[8] They also were not roomy, and would have barely had room for the general. Nevertheless, Pompey's son is thought to have ridden in his chariot 61 BC.[9] This seems like Pompey is trying to share the glory with his son in order to promote the young man's career

Finally, and probably most importantly, Pompey wore his triumphal clothes at the two-day games to commemorate his Triumph in 61. Pompey broke tradition and was allowed to wear triumphal clothes at certain public occasions. The temporary glory of the triumph was becoming a more permanent occasion;

---

[8] Beard 2007: 221.
[9] Beard 2007: 20.

Pompey was able to maintain his divine status, and with public permission.

Although not all of these incidents are directly relevant to the progression toward making a man a God in Rome, they do indicate the way that even the important and sacred traditions of the triumph could be overturned. The willingness of the Senate, the people, and the individual politicians to allow such changes partly explains how Rome slowly moved toward the acceptance of a divine status for their leaders. What does this mean for the normal everyday individual attempting to get their personal brand out there? It shows importance of taking as big action as possible and being everywhere. Also, it shows importance of observing tee individuals or in this case gods, which you need to position yourself with so that it helps to raise your own standing in the eyes of the public. They are not quite as willing to believe that you are a God anymore, though if you ask some rappers, they will beg to differ, but it can be very effective to see your name over and over again.

The Importance of Merchandise
Memory is very important to triumph; some might forget, others might have never experienced it. Divinity is only as great as its memory in the minds of the citizenry; they must be reminded constantly, lest they forget. It is the campaign of propaganda that makes Late Republic politicians and generals great, even more so than their actions. Pompey was no different than other politicians of his time; he needed to remind the populace of his great, even divine, exploits, images to last beyond the day of triumph itself.

An important technique that Pompey uses to memorialize his military exploits is to mint coins in memory of his triumphs, in order to remind those that witnessed the triumph what they had experienced. The coins had *magnus* printed on them, and the reverse side had Pompey in his triumphal chariot.[10] For his own personal remembrance, Pompey created a signet ring, on which were the three trophies of

---

[10] Beard 2007: 19, fig. 3.

triumph, reminding all those that opened his letters of his greatness.[11] If you are looking for a modern example, look at all the merchandise that Grant Cardone puts out, such as wristbands, so that he is remembered again and again.

In addition to coins, Pompey also builds more significant memorials to himself. The most notable is his theater, which, importantly, included in its complex a temple to Venus. She is especially important to Romans since she is mother of Aeneas, the founder of the nation. Pompey constructed the theatre after his first triumph in 61 BC, the temple was controversial in its day because it was a monument to a ruler very much in the Greek tradition of a ruler cult. Think of this like high-level entrepreneurs that donate money to causes such as buildings and adding their names to them.

The theatre was not his only monument promoting his links to the gods. Pompey also built a temple to Hercules, an important connection to Greek culture

---

[11] Beard 2007: 15.

and a link to a mortal who became a god.[12] Pompey's repair of the temple of Minerva is another way in which he promotes himself and associates himself with the gods.

Julius Caesar

Caesar, born in 100 BC, began his rapid ascent to the top of the Roman political world starting around 63 BC. Though originally working in coordination with Pompey and Crassus in the so-called First Triumvirate (Think of it like an 80's super group of generals) starting in 60 BC, he eventually came into conflict with Pompey, especially after the death of Crassus in 53 BC. The two were officially military opponents following Caesar's crossing of the Rubicon River in January of 49 BC when Pompey was given command of the army to oppose Caesar's march on Rome. It was, of course, Caesar who becomes the victor in the battle to be seen as a God. Caesar's connection to Venus, founder of the Julian family and mother of Aeneas, the founder of Rome,

---

[12] Beard, North, Price 1998: 122-3.

was the most important factor towards the achievement of divinity.

When Caesar and Pompey become enemies, an issue with Pompey's theater complex arises because of the temple of Venus. She is the family god of the Julii, and thus through a connection to Venus the Ancestor, Gaius *Julius* Caesar has a greater connection to this important Roman goddess. Regardless of the devotion Pompey shows to the goddess, Caesar will always have a direct link to her.[13] The most grandiose monument to an individual in Rome is, therefore, just as important as a monument to Caesar as it is to the man who built it. Whereas Pompey has a few tenuous links to the divinized Alexander the Great and builds a temple to honor Venus, Caesar can trace his lineage to Venus and her semi-divine son, Aeneas.

Caesar later built his own temple to Venus in 48 BC, Venus the Ancestor. Caesar was also given the right to adorn his own home as if it were a temple, as well as

---

[13] Plutarch, *Pompey*: 68.

being given his own priest while he was alive.[14]

Caesar, like Pompey, takes the wearing of the triumphal garments to a new level. Whereas Pompey had received permission to wear the clothes of triumph at certain public, Caesar got permission to wear the clothes of triumph at all public events.[15] This is proof that the temporary glory of the triumph was becoming more permanent; it was becoming not just a day of glory, but rather it was becoming the worship of men.[16] This shows that Pompey had made an effect, but Caesar just plain did a better job. As a personal brand, you always need to stay on top of what is happening in pop culture and your brand may need to make changes to stay on the forefront.

Caesar celebrated four triumphs at once in 46 BC.[17] The total of four at once was unprecedented and the only thing that

---

[14] Beard, North, Price 1998: 140.
[15] Beard, North, Price 1998: 143.
[16] Beard, North, Price 1998: 143.
[17] Appian, *Roman History*: 2.101.

could compete with Pompey's "conquest of the world." Moreover, Caesar exceeded the love Pompey garnered from the people with the outright purchase of their adoration: Caesar provided Rome with 60,500 silver talents, almost tripling Pompey's 20,000 silver talents from his settlement of the East in 63 BC.[18] Caesar surpassed Pompey in the greatness of his triumph, and, to end all debate, defeated him in the Battle of Pharsalus in 48 BC.

Caesar outdoes all of his predecessors in the movement toward becoming a God by claiming supernatural powers c. 44 BC.[19] Even though he does not achieve the status of a god until his death in 44 BC, Caesar's moves are far more aggressive than those of Pompey – but this bold declaration, along with most of Caesar's successes in his self-promotion, are probably not possible without the groundwork laid by Pompey.

Pompey died on the shores of Egypt where he had fled after his loss in Greece.

---

[18] Plutarch, *Pompey*: 45.3. Appian, *Roman History*: 2.102.

[19] Zanker 1992: 24.

Neither he, nor Caesar, lived to see the culmination of their efforts at self-promotion. Caesar was assassinated in 44 BC at the foot of a statue of Pompey in the Theater of Pompey and after his death that the Cult of Divine Julius was established through the efforts of his adopted heir, Octavian (given the title Augustus by the Senate in 27 BC). Neither Caesar nor Pompey enjoyed divinity in life, but the efforts of each helped to set the foundations for Augustus who not only established the cult of his adoptive father but also set up the anticipation for his own deification.[20]

Divine Branding: The God Blueprint
Augustus was well aware of how important it was to be thought a god. He was also smart enough to look at what works, he saw what he father and Pompey did correct and did the best he could to create a combination of the two. This may be one of the biggest A / B tests in history but allowed him to see what works, just like this, you need to observe

---

[20] Appian, *Roman History*. 2.117

what is happening in your space and you will be able to actually create what is looked for in your space. For example, when he was in Egypt, Augustus famously wished to see the tomb of Alexander the Great. Egypt was a land where the where even Alexander's successors, continued the ancient practice whereby the pharaoh was worshipped as a god.

As it was for Pompey, a connection to Alexander the Great was among the most important factors for Augustus in his self-promotion. An established connection to Aeneas and to Venus helped as well in so far as Octavian was a member of the Julii and the adopted son of Caesar. Through his monumentalized connection to Venus the Victorious, Pompey could only keep a connection to Venus as long as he was victorious, but a connection to Venus The Ancestor is something Augustus could not lose; he would always be a descendant of Venus.

Like Pompey, Augustus used monuments to promote himself. In his forum, completed in 2 BC, Augustus linked himself to the apotheosized Aeneas and

Romulus, along with other great Roman heroes and the god Zeus-Ammon. Ammon is particularly interesting since this god's oracle is the one that declared Alexander to be the Son of God. Augustus's great new forum was a monument to himself, through which Romans would be reminded in many different ways of his connections to myth and the gods. The forum was a new official meeting place for Romans to conduct business, public ceremony, and important matters of the state. More than Pompey's theatre, this forum was a place that Romans would frequent and be reminded – on a daily basis – of Augustus's links to divine figures and heroes from the glorious days of Rome's past.[21]

Just as Pompey did, Augustus received his first honors at a young age (for example, he became consul in his twentieth year), but the difference is he kept these honors for life and his honors went far beyond the usual and customary titles.[22] Augustus's long climb to total supremacy

---

[21] Zanker 1992: 79-82. For image of forum: Zanker 1992: 80, fig. 61.
[22] Suetonius, *Augustus*: 27.1.

in Rome, once achieved, and was hardly threatened. His competition was ruthlessly eliminated and he survived any conspiracies, consolidating his power and his status as the son of the deified Caesar throughout his sole rule from about 31 BC to his death in AD 14. He received his title, Augustus, from the Senate in 16 January 27 BC, making his full title *Imperator Caesar Divi Filius Augustus* (the Ruler Caesar Augustus, son of god). Like Pompey, Augustus used coins to promote himself, printing "divi filius" on certain coins printed after the deification of Julius Caesar

He established the cult of *Divus Juliu* starting with the funeral games he organized for Julius Caesar on the 20th - 30th, therefore his father Julius was now a God. With the establishment of Caesar's divinity, Augustus worked on his own. Taking his lead from Pompey, Augustus built a temple to Apollo on the Palatine Hill, making the temple part of his own palace; the house was very much, like Pompey's Theater, a temple to himself.

Augustus takes his connection with Apollo a step further through the rather curious dinner parties that he is known to have had. The dinners were for the twelve gods, at which his guest would dress and play the part of a different god.[23] Augustus always played the part of Apollo, Apollo the Tormentor. Alexander also considered himself to be the son of Apollo after his experience at Delphi, during which the god addresses Alexander as his son.[24]

Official mythology was an attempt by Augustus to connect himself better with Rome's past; it was an attempt to legitimize the rule of the Julian dynasty.[25] There was no precedent in Roman history to connect with Apollo, but there are attempts to connect with Jupiter through the Roman triumph.

Augustus also paid a great deal of attention to the triumph. Its grandness helped portray a larger than life

---

[23] Suetonius, *Augustus*: 70.
[24] Plutarch, *Alexander*: 14.6-8.
[25] Zanker 1992: 193.

individual, which helped promote Augustus's divine propaganda. He had regular triumphs for at least thirty generals, and he gave triumphal regalia to a greater number.[26] It would seem that though the triumph brought him to this point, he it trying to dilute its value so that no others might be brought to his high level of popularity in order to challenge his authority.[27]

Again taking his lead from Pompey, Augustus creates his own connection with the great king Alexander, through his own seal. His seal a first was sphinx, but a second version of his seal was an emblem of Alexander the Great.[28] Augustus would later create yet another seal once he is well established in his rule, but his attempts to connect with Alexander in the early phases of his rule are significant, following directly in the footsteps of Pompey.

---

[26] Suetonius, *Augustus*: 38.1.

[27] For discussions of the way Augustus preserved his glory and diminished that of others see Syme 1939:404–405; Campbell 348–51, 358–59; Hickson; Mattern 200–202; and Sailor 333.

[28] Suetonius, *Augustus*: 50.

It is important to understand the significance of the actions of Pompey. The Romans acknowledged a respect for Alexander before Pompey, but the love of Alexander seems to culminate with Pompey. Before Pompey, Rome was not ready to accept a cult to a man like Alexander or Pompey himself, but after a long and slow process and the bold actions of men like Marius, Pompey finally and fully breached the barriers of Roman resistance to human divinity and prepared the people of Rome to accept a divine leader. Rome passed the point where it could be ruled by men, and with Augustus and his successors, only a god could rule a city so great on the world stage.

Though this is an extreme example, when applied to the modern media, it shows how the modern spin machine works. Your personal brand is battle of press, positioning and keeping your name known on a daily basis. A podcast can be what takes your personal brand to another place because you have pieces of content coming out several times a week, which we will see later can be repurposed in many different ways given the correction action plan.

5

What Can A Podcast Do For Your Personal Brand?

"A brand for a company is like a reputation for a person. You earn reputation by trying to do hard things well."
– *Jeff Bezos*

Podcasts area a 100% free product, and if you ask some that tried the paid subscription method, it really doesn't work. On the contrary, they are something that you can download and listen to at your leisure. So why do I put so much value in a completely free product, that as a host, you have to pay to produce? I say so because of the effect and the reach that you can have with a podcast. The audience is growing, and it has an ability to lift you from obscurity better than anything else; that is if you do it correctly.

According to podcast host Libsyn, total podcast downloads grew from 1.9 billion to 2.6 billion from 2013 to 2014; that's huge growth upside. Not to be outdone, there was incredible growth again in 2015, with at least 21% of the US population — nearly 57 million individuals — downloading a show at least once per month.

To put it in perspective, 15% of the population listens to Spotify, the top music streaming service that added podcasts last month, in the same interval.

Podcast listeners are highly mobile, with 64% of users listening on a smartphone or tablet. Being that the average commute in America is 25 minutes, there is an audience just waiting for your content. With all this, it totally makes sense that 4 times as many audio podcasts are downloaded as video podcasts. For the most part, podcast listeners are doing something else while they listen, which allow you to become part of their commute or workout.

I'm not going to lie to you — there are challenges that exist in creating a show. These include creating content at least once every week, editing and creating a final file (done right, it's time-consuming) not to mention having to promote something brand new. But there is still a lot of value to be had.

In comparison to blogging, significantly less people are podcasting due to the time commitment it takes not only to execute, but also to do in a professional manner. This means less competition in the space, giving you a greater opportunity to be found and heard.

So, what can a podcast do for your personal brand?

1. Creating a Opinion Leader (OL) Status

Marketing guru, Seth Godin, has often referred to the idea of creating a *tribe,* a group of people that follow and digest everything you create, and audio is perfect for creating this effect. Audio creates a relationship which blogging and the written word cannot duplicate. Listeners know your voice, they know how you communicate on topics, and it also helps to position you as an opinion leader.

Media expert, Kevin Kelly, has expanded on this idea in his article "1,000 True Fans," in which he talks about creating not just listeners but raving fans or "evangelists" for your brand.

True fans will share your message with others, and create a larger sphere of influence for your brand. Being that audio content is easily digestible it's ripe for the creation of opinion leader status.

2. Audio Content is Easier for Your

Audience to Assimilate
Podcast listeners are often doing something else while consuming content — be it working out, commuting or drudging through paperwork. The medium allows for your content to be consumed in places that it's just not possible to consume the written word.

When it comes down to it, listening takes less effort on the part of the consumer, and producing a podcast takes your company to where consumers are going.

3. You can get 8 Free Weeks of Promotion
If you have done a good enough job in promoting the launch of your show, then iTunes will promote you in a section of their catalog called "New and Noteworthy." What this means is free advertising for your show, in front of the perfect audience for it.

To give you an idea of the numbers, John Lee Dumas of *Entrepreneur on Fire Podcast*, received 2,700 (81,000 per month) downloads per day during promotion and 900 per day after — showing the true value in iTunes free promotion. Dumas' show has continued to grow and currently receives 1.5 million downloads per month, or about 50,000 per day. Free promotion was enough to get John his 1,000 true fans to keep his platform growing.

4. Re-purposing of Content Allows a Wider Audience to be Reached

A podcast allows you to create content that can be shared in several places, not just as audio but also in the written word and as video as well. Most podcasters use their audio episodes to create a blog post called "Show Notes," — these are either a transcript or the most important points and links from the episode, and will even go as far as to make the audio interview into a video to reach an even wider YouTube audience.

By re-purposing you can create one piece of content and feature it different ways to reach a wider audience. We will get into how exactly that you can do that in a later chapter.

5. It Can be a Valuable Networking Tool
The great majority of podcasts are conducted as interviews, and this plays a few vital roles in the episodes' promotion. First off it's a valuable networking tool for the interviewer, it allows him to connect with opinion leaders in their space and use the opinion leader's name as positioning to make the interviewer and brand appear even stronger and more prominent.

And if you're good, in many cases your OL will want to promote it to their email list as well, growing your listener and fan base wider by virtue of offering valuable content to more new people not already on your list.

Podcasting a medium is quickly becoming crowded, with almost 13,000 podcasts added from 2015 to 2016. But getting your voice in now will allow your company to hold a valuable piece of Internet real estate, and allow you to build a platform in the ever-changing future of media. The question really is not *if* your company should start a podcast, but rather *when*.

6

Starting Your Podcast

"Purpose is one thing that drives me everyday. Find yours and you will be willing to die doing it."
-Grant Cardone

The most vital thing about your podcast is the concept that it puts out. What I mean by that is a purpose that the audience doesn't just buy into, but will become passionate about. Something that there is such an emotional connection with, that it can really have a wide stretching effect and actually communicate what it means.

Your Show Title

My show title and my purpose very closely related, and though I'd like to say took a lot of time and thinking, it did not. My show is called Create Your Own Life, and for me is actually very personal. After leaving my job teaching, I had a conversation with my dad in which I told him that I wanted to create my own life. I had tried many different types of businesses, in addition to teaching, and had decided I would start some online type of business, not that I had any expertise. I read an article on INC.com about hashtagging and that it would be beneficial to have one hashtag that I used in common between all my Instagram posts. I started using #CreateYourLife, it got the point across of that I was feeling, and wasn't being used by other people.

When it later came time to start a podcast I decided to call it the "Create Your Life" podcast, but that name was already taken. So, the new name was "Create Your Own Life," little did I know that the reflexive nature of the name made it a significantly better name than I had planned using. The next thing I had to decide was the purpose of what I was doing, but that took a little thinking and several revisions, even after the show was active, before I arrived at my current purpose.

Currently, the purpose of the show is to help the listener to "create life on their own terms." I help the listener to do so by studying people that have created life on their own terms through an interview format. The show title has worked so well that people like Grant Cardone, Tucker Max and Jim Mathers have all remarked during their interviews how much sense it meant to them and their lives' stories.

The Format
You show format for the most part, should not be that difficult. As you can guess by now, to work with my method, you will be doing interviews. For doing this, make my calls over Skype with ECAMM Call Recorder to record them. Interviews come down to figuring out questions for the guest that help to tell the type of story that aligns with your show's purpose. All of those questions should be very open-ended with you facilitating them in the answers. In terms

of putting interviews together for each guest, I have found that listening to other shows at 2x speed has been the best preparation method for me.

My preparation has changed a lot since I started podcasting. Early on, if I did not have a list of 25 questions, I would not have enough to keep a guest talking for 30-40 minutes. The more interviews I did, the better I got at interviewing and I learned just how important to a good show a good quality interviewer can be.

The interviewer should be someone that is very interested in the guest, and come from the viewpoint of what the audience would want to know. I found that once it become more of a conversation, with a bit of finesse, I came up with a few topics based on the guest's life experience and preparation for interviews became significantly less. I cannot stress enough how important it is to practice your skill as an interviewer. It's so much different than you expect once you really get in the game.

The Launch Plan

There is a difference of opinion in the podcast world whether or not each show should have an "episode 0." This is the first episode of your show, quite short, usually under 10 minutes, and goes over why the show is happening, its content and its publishing schedule. I'm basing this purely off stats, but my episode 0 does a decent number of downloads every month to the point that I am sure new listeners go back to it to see what the show is all about. To really let new people go back to the purpose of your show it's very important to have this episode to go back to. The beautiful thing about it is that you can re-record this episode whenever needed to help and hook new listeners. The caveat to this is that when publishing the replacement, put the date as before all of your current episode, otherwise it will show up as the newest episode of your podcast.

There is also a difference of opinion dealing with how many episodes with which you should publish your show. The typical idea was 3 shows, but I tend to agree with Nathan Latka on show length.

The total content submitted to iTunes should be at least 3 episodes or 2 total hours of content. So, if you have a 15-minute show, then you should start with 8 episodes. The point here is that 2 hours of content is enough to hook a new listener.

Your Review Flurry
Once your show is live and available to listen, it is time to get new listeners to subscribe to and review you podcast. The reason for this action is to get into the iTunes "New & Noteworthy" section where your show is then put in front of millions of eyes that could possibly become your audience; all for free. I will go over the strategy that I used, though I was just trying to take as much action as possible and it wasn't well organized. If you have an established business with a large database, this is a much easier action, though it's more than just sending an email and hoping there has to be a bit of making sure the reviews actually happen.

When starting my podcast I took a lot of action to avoid obscurity, your biggest enemy in getting started. I will give you the idea of what I did, these numbers are rounded rather than the exact numbers that I did, but the level of action is in the thousands. I took a lot of action on LinkedIn, though I caution you that there is a method to it, and too much without knowing the method can get your account blocked. Facebook does have a limit as well and it's not smart to drop your link in groups without asking because it will result in getting you blocked from Facebook. Given that fact, I relied on Facebook Messenger, but even that has its limits, as I was blocked from sending the same link somewhere near 500. If you smart and can figure out some other way around it, then go for it, but I advise you to know the people that you are asking for reviews or you could end up with some negative ones, which can be dangerous. I did most of these with a bit.ly link to make less text that I had to send.

My Action Plan
1. Text Messages with link: 700

2. Personal Emails: 250

3. Mailchimp Emails: 190

4. LinkedIn Messages: 2,700

5. Facebook Messages: 500

6. Phone Calls: 100

7. People in Public Places: 50

As you can see, the amount of action, especially if you are not well known, is a high level of communication. The number above is 4,040. A huge amount of communication to get 100 reviews, but no one knew whom I was and I was willing to do whatever it took to really get my message out there. I want you to understand that you can win, but you need to work really hard with very big numbers to do so.

The appendix to this chapter is a time line from a high level perspective, meaning that it covers the big actions that need to be done. You will have to go back over what we have covered and what we have yet to cover in order to really put together your exact action plan.

Appendix 1: Podcast Launch Timeline

I. Pick Your Topic.

II. Pick your title.
   a. Make Sure the Title is Succinct.
   b. Have a good purpose and tagline.

III. Have website setup to represent what you are doing and matching social media pages.

IV. Schedule guests, storing up enough content for at least one month.

V. Develop your launch plan; pay special attention to the first episodes to go to iTunes.

VI. Have your podcast hosting setup; find out what link you host wants to go to iTunes.

VII. Submit your podcast to iTunes.

VIII. Wait 2-3 days, checking each day if it is visible in iTunes. You will be told when it is available but no searchable.

IX. Get as many people as you can to review the show, I worked to get almost 5,000 people to do so, ending up with about 100 reviews.

X. Write press release and submit to various news sources.

7

How to Reach Anyone, the Tried and True Method

"A person's success in life can usually be measured by the number of uncomfortable conversations he or she is willing to have."
                    -Tim Ferriss

As I have stated, before, an interview show is the way to go, unless of course you have boundless amounts of unique content already created. In my experience, the media standing of whom you are interviewing is important, for the reason that it creates excitement and it helps with search traffic to what you are doing. As we have previously mentioned, positioning based on whom you are interviewing is important as well.

The first thing I start with is creating a large list, 100 or more is a good base number to start with. I made a list of the 100 people that I most admired when I got started, because to really have big success, you have to aim big. At a certain point, you will run out of names to think of, but there is a way to handle that.

I handled the problem of lack of more names by searching Amazon books of the topic I was studying: entrepreneurship. To give credit where its due, I got the idea from Andrew Ferebee of the Knowledge for Men Podcast. With this in your tool kit, the number of names that you can come up with is almost infinite. When I hear podcasters say that it's difficult to book guests, I find that they just aren't dealing with answers, just problems.

After you have made your list, next it's up to you to find out how to contact these individuals. I found that contact forms on websites were just not the best place to contact the people that I wanted to interview. The best way to operate was to right to the person that I wanted to interview.

I did a lot of guessing early on including their name at their domain or initials. Each time, I waited to see if an email bounced back to me, telling me that the email I tried was not the correct one. As you can imagine, I spent a lot of time you sending emails and hoping. That initial set of emails took me about 8 hours to write, and at the end of this chapter, you will see a rough format of how I approached people. I actually found email was actually the best way to approach people. Given all the phone calls I had made in my earlier sales career, I had decided that I did not want to make any call, so email would have to work.

The current method I have used saves a lot of time and had a much better success rate with contacting many of the people I have wanted to speak to. This method has developed from two separate conversations that I had with Nathan Chan and Jeremy Adams. There have been a few guests that I have contacted by message on Facebook fan pages, but the numbers of those that action is possible for is very low.

Contacting A-List Celebrities

First I start with a person that I want to interview, if they are super famous, for example Jamie Foxx, then I know that their website is not the way to contact them. His or her site is most likely managed by someone that has nothing to do with the person that I want to interview. Someone on this level most likely has a Public Relations firm that represents him or her. So, your next step would be doing some Google work to find out who represents them. There are a lot of fake "Contact Any Celebrity" sites, don't fall for them. If you have gotten lucky, like I did when wanting to interview P90X creator Tony Horton, then the PR firm will help you get scheduled to interview the requested expert.

This method does not work every single time, as some a-list celebrities want to make it very difficult to contact them, so it may take some time and networking with others to score the interview. A great way to interview politicians is to find out who is their campaign manager is or to find out whom their chief of staff is; that's your way through the door there.

The Email Guess Method
This method has gotten way better over time. As I said before, it started with me just trying things or the Gmail Plugin Rapportive, which isn't quite that reliable, and after long periods of time having results. The improved method works like this. I find the person in question's website, the head over to emailhunter.co. When I type in the domain, it spits out results, if the person I want to contact is included in the results, unless of course you want to email Tim Ferriss, then I'm all set.

If the name in question is not there, then Email Hunter gives you the format of all the emails on that site for example FirstInitial_LastName@domain.com. Then, you are able to guess names with a lot more insight, than just trying and seeing what works. It was this method that got me in contact with Donald Trump's campaign manager.

As you can see, there is quite a bit to getting great guests on your show, but you may not get them the first time around. Just as in sales, following up with guests or PR firms is very important to getting a guest to appear on your show. The individual that I most wanted to interview took following up every month for almost a year to interview. Want great guests? Don't be shortsighted and stay consistently on top of communication to possible guests.

Appendix 2: My Email Templates:

Email #1

(Subject Line is important, but will have to find what works for your brand.)

Hi_____,

I'd be thrilled to have you on my podcast show *[Podcast Name Here]*, recently featured in iTunes New and Noteworthy, the #1 ranked podcast in Business and is exceeding *[Insert #]* downloads per month in addition to my blog, from over *[Insert Number]* countries.

I've been interviewing the most successful and inspiring people in the areas of life: business building, lifestyle marketing, professional athletes, authors and entrepreneurship.

A few notable speakers booked/interviewed:
[Insert 3-5 names]

Interviews are 40 minutes over Skype.

If interested, let's arrange a time together.

Best,
[Your Name]

Email #2
Hi ___,
I'm excited to have you on [Insert Name] podcast.

Click Below to Schedule a Time for Your Interview:
[Insert scheduler link here]

Checklist to a Great Show (MOST IMPORTANT):
___A bullet point list of your life and career so I have a greater idea about you to better promote you. (48 hours before I will give you the show questions)

___An external microphone OR at least your smartphone headset. Shows will cannot be conducted without mic-ing of some kind; I want you to get the most out of this!

___Your Skype ID, calls will be conducted over Skype. If you do not have it, it can be downloaded at www.skype.com.

___How can I be the most help to YOU on this interview?

Best,
[Your Name]

Email #3

Subject Line: Confirmation *[Date]* and *[Time]*

Hi _____,

Looking forward to our chat tomorrow at *[Time / Time Zone]*.

Look for a Skype request from *[Your Skype ID]*, any issues my cell is *[Your Cell Number]*.

Below is our format, please let me know if

there is anything you need help promoting! If there is anything in particular that you want to cover please let me know :)

Best,
[Your Name]

Email #4
(Sent Following Day after interview)

Hi _____,

Thank You so much for being on the [Show Name] Podcast. I hope it was as valuable to you as it will be to our audience!

Your tentative publish date is:
[Insert Date]

It is tentative because sometimes, do to unforeseen circumstances it can change. Is this date the best for what you're working on, or would there be a date close to this one, that would be better for you?

Best,

[Your Name]

PS - if you could review us in iTunes I would be ever so grateful!

[iTunes Direct Link]

Email #5
(Scheduled for 8 am with Boomerang)

Hi ___,
Your interview is LIVE and will be listened to by thousands of people all across the world from over 165 countries! I can't wait to share your success and information with them!

Help me get your episode out there by sharing with your audience. I've found that people that are already interested in what you are doing are the most helpful in getting out to people that have yet discovered you. I have had guests tell me that by sharing, it has opened up other opportunities for their brand; I want that to happen for you!

I would be honored if you would share with your audience to impact more lives with your amazing story!

Your Show's link:
[Blog Direct Link with Embedded Player]

Have a great day!
[Your Name]

8

The Podcast Production List

"The professional has learned that success, like happiness, comes as a by-product of work. The professional concentrates on the work and allows rewards to come or not come, whatever they like."

-Steven Pressfield

The following is a checklist that I put together to track my workflow through scheduling into content creation. It's the basics, as I've taken out some of the things that are difficult to explain or that I use video to train my staff on.

With everything here, you should be able to start your production and really get something moving for yourself. Though, as you can see, the process is a bit daunting, and professional help can really help you to boom it to the next level.

The following sequence takes effect after the sending of email number 1. It takes you step by step through it; though you have to fill in some of the details otherwise this could be 20 pages long.

Appendix 3: Podnast Production Checklist

I. Schedule Guest
- Guest Name: _____

- Set Date with Email # 2 / Interview DATE:_____

- Release Date:_____

- Show # _____

- Put together guest questions

- Send Email # 3 and collect Skype Name _____

- Conduct Interview

- 24 Hours After interview, send email # 4

II. File Creation

- Split video file into separate sides of conversation, if you're using ECAMM Call Recorder is a function of it. ECAMM also does MP3 conversion.

- Convert video 1 to MP3

- Convert video 2 to MP3

- Open Episode template (This is something you should have the basics, that do not change, for each show)

- Save File As… *[**Format:** Show #_Guest Name]*

- In Intro Delete episode number sound clip, record new episode sound clip to overwrite

- Drag in MP3 clip # 1

- Drag in MP3 clip # 2

- Remove "Um," "Ah," and any sections unnecessary to show production, such as side banter or long pauses.

- In Outro line, record Outro.

- Depending on what you're using (Adobe Audition is Preferred) Export your file as an MP3

III. File Tagging and Blog Entry

- Create show title, *[**Format:** Show #: Show Title — Guest Name]*

- Create a new blog post on your website to function as "Show Notes"

- Open ID3 Editor and file created in section

- In Title, Artist, Genre and Caption spaces insert information from above blog post.

- Also in ID3 Editor add show picture, I recommend custom for each show.

- Save the file and close ID3 Editor

- Log into podcast host, I recommend Libsyn

- Click upload, and upload file just tagged

- In description, paste Wordpress blog text

- In Thumbnail, upload show image used in ID3

- Click 'Schedule release / Expiration,' Click Select new release date, and set for 12:00 AM on release day.

- Click Publish

- Copy Embedded play link in Wordpress Site

- Schedule Wordpress post for 7 AM on day of release and click 'Schedule.'

V. Create Email List Broadcast
- Log into email client

- Copy text from Wordpress site blog post

- Paste into Mailer

- Schedule broadcast for 7 AM on release day.

VI. Promotion
- Send email # 5 24 hours before

- Rework copy specific to guest for email # 6

- Copy show link from [YourDomain.com], Paste into email

- Send email to Guest

- Create Instagram Promotion

- Create Pretty Link, and connect to promotion

- Launch Instagram promotion

9

The Content Repurposing Formula

"The easiest way to turn off your community members is to broadcast the same message across multiple channels. Instead, determine the kind of content that interests the members of your community in a way that is useful to them."

-Joe Pulizzi,

Entrepreneurs and businesses sometimes struggle to create enough valuable content to reach their audience — the time investment needed being one of the top gripes. However, it's just a matter of viewpoint—the door is actually wide open for someone with a focused mission who really wants to get themselves out there. The key is *creative repurposing* of content. Using some of the following methods, you can make an impact starting with just one piece of superior-quality content.

Let's make one thing very clear right up front: "repurposing content" does *not* mean you write a blog post once, then repost it ten times; that's distasteful and actually hurts SEO. Rather, here's a step-by-step method that you can try and if you do it well could be the "secret sauce" for your brand.

A lot of podcasters go wrong in thinking that they make one piece of content, their episode, and it's all over. A smart podcaster will find as many ways and places as possible to use the content so that they can blanket the online world with their episode. It takes a lot of effort to really make an effect so having your content everywhere possible is key to real success.

Blog Post:

Start by writing a really great blog post — high-end, quality content with the right citations and directed towards your public. It must be *original content;* in order to do the rest of the steps following, that's very important.

Podcast:
Create a 5-10 minute podcast based upon what you just wrote in your blog. In preparation, bullet point it out, don't be robotic, and don't be afraid to adlib a bit. Remember, now you're *speaking aloud* to a human audience, so you have to have good verbal communication *(Danger, Will Robinson!)* A good tip if you've never done this before is to practice saying it aloud a few times before you hit "record."

Video:
How this step looks depends upon what you did in the previous step. If you did your podcast as a video or movie file, which I recommend, then this step becomes a no-brainer. Other options include putting an audio file behind some sort of imagery (many video editing

softwares can do this easily) and create a video from that. Then you can upload in places such as YouTube and Vimeo.

Transcription:
There are many different options for doing this, but the point is, now you can get your original podcast / video transcribed, meaning a document of everything said in its duration. This can be used this effectively for a lead capture, as a white paper or as some sort of special report which is promoted out to your audience.

If you are taking advantage of putting videos on YouTube, then you have the ability to take advantage of the free transcription service.

Quote Graphics:
Have you seen those quote squares all over social media? They're shareable and tend to get a lot of interaction. Now that you have a transcription of everything you've just said in your audio program, it's time to create some meaningful and

shareable social content from it. Apps like Typorama are really great for this.

You may have to tweak your methods a bit and figure out the best way that this will work for you, but this is a workable blueprint on how to write something once and continue to use it while still delivering value.

If you observe a lot of big brands online, they are doing exactly the same — it's one way they're able to be in so many different places and deliver a message that really impacts.

They are repurposing a single piece of original content into several different media and formats, thus maximizing on message itself and on the time that it took to create it.

10
Podcast Tools For Success

"Technology is nothing. What's important is that you have a faith in people, that they're basically good and smart, and if you give them tools, they'll do wonderful things with them."
                            -Steve Jobs

Your personal branding program can seem a little daunting, and though we have already went through the action steps, I've put together some tools that may have already been mentioned or may be a brand new part of what we are doing.

However, with a little organization and

the right tools, not only can you get more done, you'll end up less aggravated. There's just some tasks that we have to do a lot and it would be a ton easier if we could shortcut them. For most, not doing them at all is not an option, so we look for shortcuts or different ways to get ourselves out of the way. You will find that most of the software on here is just for Mac, I hate to say it but for most part, much of the best software for recording and editing on a podcast is only for Mac. There are PC softwares, such as Pamela for PC, which records Skype calls, but they have a much higher level of difficulty in operation and lack some types of functionality.

The following will help you keep everyone on the same page, take out some monotonous steps and also keep progress moving without all your attention on it.

1 Evernote:
>This app is one that is installed on every device that you have, and when connected to the Internet, each device updates regularly. It's

like your notepad that's a lot harder to lose.

Evernote gives you the ability to keep written and audio notes on one device that appears on all your devices, be it your phone tablet or computer. It also can transform pictures to text quite accurately, a function that is great with business cards, which can be pushed to your device's contacts. I've used this app less and less and come to rely on Google Drive more often.

2 Calendly:
Scheduling can be the biggest pain, mainly because if you give date options to different people, you can never give them the same days chances are they will both select the same one. Inevitably, there's always the back and forth to hash out a date and time or rescheduling.

Calendly syncs with your device's calendar or your Google Calendar and allows people to select preapproved times set by you. You simply send someone a link, and an email with a selected time appears in your inbox and is already added to your calendar; if someone needs to reschedule Calendly will help them to do that as well; brain cells saved.

3 Boomerang:
Batching email is common way to save time on sending out mail, but there's always the chance that you want the message you are writing now to send at a later time. Boomerang syncs with your Gmail account, and gives you the option to schedule individual emails to send at a later time. Now you can still batch your email time and send something at a time when you know the receiver will have time to read it or less mail in their inbox.

4 Google Drive:
For your standard documents to you team, Google Drive is the way

to go. It allows you to store files on Google's server, in addition to running their app on your phone or computer, allowing you access without Wifi. This also combats not being able to send large files to the rest of the team; with Drive they are easily accessible and downloadable.

If you want to edit those documents on mobile, Google has other apps that you have to download in order to do that. I tend to do most of my work on desktop for that very reason.

5 Basecamp:
Running a successful podcast, which really a single person cannot do, but the organization of it can also work out to be a bit crazy. Basecamp is application that allows you to assign tasks to individuals, keep track of progress and also store relevant information such as imagery and passwords.

6 Emailhunter.co

The Shout out goes to Jeremy Adams on this little gem. It had become very quickly become my go to app, as you saw in the earlier section about my method for reaching certain high level individuals. It allows you to see known emails at domains and also the format that emails are structured at certain site, so that you can give an email address your best guess.

7 ECAMM Call Recorder

This app runs about $30 dollars but is the app has been the most important in my business. It allows for the recording of Skype calls. It outputs a file that is in QuickTime Movie format, but also includes the tools to split the files to be able to edit each person's speech and convert them into an MP3 file.

8 Skype

Skype is software that allows you to

make video calls or phone calls over the Internet or depending how busy you guest is, their smart phone. I have heard others talk about nightmares with using Skype, but in almost 200 calls, I have only dropped less than 10 times; 4 were during the same call due to a poor connection.

9 Zencastr

I have heard great things about this app, and as of the time of writing this, it's a free app. Zencastr is a recording software that runs through web browser and records natively on each person's computer rather than voice over IP like Skype, it takes a lot of the issues of Wi-Fi out of the equation. I haven't really used this one mainly out of being comfortable with Skype, but this sounding like the best future option to go with.

10   Envisage.io

It's important to keep stats of all the

important things in your business, such as communications, downloads and all other types of stats. It's important to track all aspects of your business by statistics, and that's exactly what I do. This is more optional, but It would be stupid not to use this software.

11 **Wi-Fi**

This may sound like a no brainer, but having really good Wi-Fi is super important to have a good sounding show. Otherwise, audio can come out sounding electronic or tinny. Additionally, it can make you appear unprofessional to the people that you are interviewing.

12 **Libsyn**

There are many, many podcast hosts out on the World Wide Web, but I have only used Libsyn and Soundcloud. When put side by side, Soundcloud is significantly cheaper, but Libsyn has so many more options, including better statistics, that it is hands down the better of the two that I have tried.

You need a podcast host because without it, there is nowhere to put your files. Most of them reset on a monthly basis, which allows to have hundreds of episodes, helping you to have better SEO in iTunes and on your blog.

13 Pond5

I have heard that there are other companies out there that do what Pond5 does, but I continue to use them, mainly out of familiarity. It is a royalty free music site which is where I buy all my sound buffers and intro / outro music from. It depends what type of file you buy, but for the most part I have paid $20 per file.

14 Adobe Audition

The beautiful thing about Adobe is that for $50 per month you get access to every app you that they make. It goes without saying that you will need more than just Audition, but Photoshop and InDesign as well; both of which are included in your membership.

15 **Final Cut X**
I do all my video editing in Final Cut and it makes it super easy to make a video easily uploaded to YouTube. I find the best format to export as is "Apple Devices," this creates a file that is still pretty large but still easily added to YouTube.

Productivity all comes down to understanding the value of your time, and more time is added cost to a podcast program. Cutting down on wasted time and cost will help you add more to your bottom line and also allow you to produce more content which is an absolute most for rising above all the noise in the podcasting space.

11

Gear for a Professional Podcast

"The magic can happen in a studio. Special things can happen in a recording studio, even though it may seem like a clinical environment from the outside looking in."
-Benny Green

The following pieces of gear are what I use to get very good sound at a pretty low cost. I don't have any deals set up with any of these companies at the time of writing this. Though, as much as I like these, I can't guarantee that I won't at some point.

I have been through a few different setups for recording, but this setup has been what I have found to be the most workable and also the best for creating professional level sound.

1. **Audio Technica ATR 2100:**
   I have used several different types of microphones, Samson Meteor being the main one that I did most of my early work on, but it died pretty quickly and customer service only answers email and took 4 months to get back to me. For the Price, the Audio Technica device works very well and as a condenser USB mic it's the best you can get without have to buy a lot more gear and upgrade microphones.

2. **NEWER Boom Arm:**
   I honestly bought the boom arm because it was cool and I wanted to feel like I was on the radio. However, looking back, it's made the actual process feel a lot more

professional and made the sound quality better because of how the mic can be positioned. However, without a shock mount, the two are almost impossible to connect.

3. **Dragon Pad Pop Filter**
   The pop filter grabs excess air that comes out on certain syllables, such as "S" and "P." You may think this is an excess piece, but it really makes a huge difference in recording quality and actually having a pop filter is night and day difference between the two.

4. **Samson SP01 Shock Mount**
   A shock mount makes it so you mic does jump every time you move or put your hand down on the desk. You'd be surprised how much a mic will pick up without having a shock mount to catch any excess movement. Also, when using a boom arm and the ATR2100, the two do not connect without a shock mount.

5. **MacBook Pro**

Everything I recommend in this book only works on Mac, so this is why I recommend a MacBook. There's all different sorts of models, so it depends on what's best for your business, but the newer, the better so that the laptop can keep up with software; especially the Adobe products which require a lot of hard drive use.

When I got started, I couldn't afford a new computer and spent $130 to put a new solid-state hard drive into it, which allowed most functionality, except recording my interviews as videos.

6. **Behringer HPS3000 Studio Headphones**
For the most part, any type of studio headphones will work because they block out the guest's voice from getting picked up by your mic. I prefer the Behringer because they always seem to have good sound at a very low cost in comparison.

The above is the minimum amount of audio gear that you need to get started. There's a lot more that you can do with minimal improvement but it's not really necessary and there's no need to put that in the way of getting you started. Though you can use thing like smartphone headphones for your microphone, there is a world of difference in using a real mic and that does a lot to position you a professional. That being said, spend the money to get started in the right way and give yourself a real chance to win.

12

Finding True Meaning in Success

A podcast can be a great decision for your brand, especially if you already have one. Audio just has a way of creating an effect so quickly; so much more so than any other medium. Applying these methods will create success for you. I remember back to before I started the Create Your Own Life Podcast, I started another show called Rock Your Life. I had no idea what the audience wanted, no idea on how to create a show and no idea and of course no idea about iTunes New and Noteworthy. Even worse, I have no plan and because of that, the show never made it to 20 episodes; zero effect.

The difference the second time around is that not only did I have a plan, I studied what worked for other people and then I was able to make a much larger impact than I could have dreamed would occur. You don't have to fail to figure out the how or spend lots of time figuring it all out. We can do it for you or you can apply these concepts and do it for yourself. Its up to you and you have the power.

Who is your audience? Who are your opinion leaders? What can you solve in their life? Don't do into it blind and don't always think that you are the expert. You may have a ton of experience but the online world doesn't know it yet. Interview others to share in their succes, then once you online brand is established, its time to share that success with the world.

Success in this program for you will me

more sales, more press and more opportunities, but don't let it stop there. Let the success you achieve mean more for you and your brand.

Success means a lot of different things to many people. Over the last few years, after starting a podcast, I have had the pleasure of asking hundreds highly successful people what that single word means to them. There's an interesting correlation in their answers. They have given at least one of two answers; success for them is the ability help others or it means freedom. However, when you boil it all down, it actually all comes down to freedom.

Freedom in business is not in the sense that they do not have to work, that's not the point. But it offers them choices. They have the ability to choose when, where and with whom they work. When you look at it that way, which is really the greatest luxury.

Many of us are not at that level yet where we have the ability to tell a certain customer that we are not interested in working with them.

So true freedom earned from success does not mean that you do not have to work but rather you have choices. Now, deciding what to do with that time is what really decides it's worth.

When you really look at it, down at its core, time is all that we really have. Our success, whatever it may be, give us the ability to be present with our families or to help others chase and reach their dreams.

Albert Einstein said it best "Seek not to be a person of success but a person on value." What will you create or how will you give value; it is in that, which you will truly find success. When you earn the ability to have choice, how will you spend the only true capital that each of us owns, time?